CRYPTO REVOLUTION

An Introduction to Cryptocurrency, NFTs, Metaverse, and Decentralized Finance

NANA BOATENG

TABLE OF CONTENTS

Chapter 1

WHAT ARE CRYPTOCURRENCIES

Cryptocurrency is digital money with the same function as physical cash: it serves as trade. People may use cryptocurrencies to pay for products and services, but it is best recognized as a speculative investment asset.

Cryptocurrency, often known as "crypto," employs blockchain technology to record transactions in a ledger system. The essential feature of this technology is that it can be seen publicly. Still, anyone cannot modify or control it, making cryptocurrencies safe for online transactions and virtually hard to counterfeit.

Individual coin ownership records are held in a digital ledger, a computerized database that uses strong encryption to safeguard transaction records, regulate currency production, and verify coin ownership transfers. Despite their name, cryptocurrencies are not necessarily considered currencies in the traditional sense. While various categorical treatments, such as classification as commodities, securities, and currencies, have been applied, cryptocurrencies are generally viewed as a distinct asset class in practice. Several cryptosystems utilize validators to keep the currency operating. In a proof-of-stake system, token owners put up their tokens as collateral. They get authority over the token in proportion to the amount pledged in exchange. Token holders often obtain more ownership in the token overtime via network fees, newly issued tokens, or other similar compensation mechanisms.

Cryptocurrency does not exist physically (unlike paper money) and is not often issued by a central body. Unlike central bank digital money, cryptocurrencies often use decentralized control (CBDC). It is considered centralized when a cryptocurrency is coined or created before release or a single issuer issues it. When decentralized governance is used, each cryptocurrency runs using distributed ledger technology, most often a blockchain, which serves as a public financial transaction database.

A cryptocurrency is a transferable digital asset or digital form of money that lives solely online and is based on blockchain technology. As the name implies, Cryptocurrencies employ encryption to authenticate and safeguard transactions. There are presently over a thousand distinct cryptocurrencies in use throughout the globe, and advocates view them as the way to a more equitable future economy.

Bitcoin, the first decentralized cryptocurrency, was published as open-source software in 2009. Many more cryptocurrencies have been launched after the introduction of bitcoin.

HOW MANY CRYPTOCURRENCIES EXIST?

Today, hundreds of cryptocurrencies are openly traded, and more are constantly being added to the market. However, many of these cryptocurrencies are unknown and have little trading activity. Bitcoin (BTC-USD), Ethereum (ETH-USD), Litecoin (LTC-USD), and Bitcoin Cash are examples of popular, extensively traded cryptocurrencies (BCH-USD).

HOW DOES THE VALUE OF A CRYPTOCURRENCY INCREASE?

By July 2021, the total value of all cryptocurrencies had surpassed $1 trillion. The value of cryptocurrency, like other currencies, is primarily determined by the currency's supply and demand in the market. However, unlike conventional currencies, cryptocurrency is neither issued by a central bank nor backed by a government. As a result, monetary policy, inflation, and economic growth do not affect the value of cryptocurrencies.

Other factors that may impact the value of a cryptocurrency include the cost of production or the mining process, the supply and demand for rival cryptocurrencies, the exchanges on which it trades, and any governing rules or limits imposed on it.

THE BENEFITS AND DRAWBACKS OF CRYPTOCURRENCY

There has been no lack of financial media coverage of cryptocurrency's quick rise and acceptance. However, like with other forms of financial assets, some substantial risks and downsides come with the potential for development and rewards.

The Benefits of Cryptocurrency Anonymity:

Cryptocurrency transactions are fully anonymous, advantageous for people who value their privacy.

Although transactions are anonymous, data is maintained on an open ledger utilizing blockchain technology. This implies that information is visible and accessible to the public at all times.

Decentralization:

Because cryptocurrency is neither issued nor backed by a central bank nor a federal government, there is no government intervention or monetary policy influence.

Possibility of fast gain:

Bitcoin, the popular cryptocurrency, has seen numerous brief moments of tremendous gains, such as the first four months of 2021 when its price more than quadrupled before dropping again. In addition, some of the highest daily profits in cryptocurrency have exceeded 200 percent.

Cons of Cryptocurrency Price Volatility:

While rapid gains are a huge draw for many prospective investors, swift and drastic drops in v are also possible value. A recent example is Bitcoin's 50% price collapse in only two months, from April to June 2021.

Excessive production costs:

Many coin kinds demand massive amounts of power and other resources to mine. For example, the bulk of the expenses associated with Bitcoin is represented by the energy necessary to mine it.

Regulatory constraints:

While cryptocurrencies are usually legal in many industrialized nations, central governments do not legally control the currency. Investing in a cryptocurrency will be risky until federal governments accept and regulate it in the same manner as fiat currencies like the US dollar.

Coins at risk of being lost:

Many cryptocurrencies, such as Bitcoin, need the use of a private key to get access to currency tokens kept in a digital "wallet." If you lose your key or your computer hardware breaks, you lose your tokens, which are irrecoverable.

CRYPTOCURRENCY HISTORY

In 1983, an American cryptographer named David Chaum devised ecash, an anonymous cryptographic electronic money. Later, in 1995, he implemented Digicash, an early sort of cryptographic electronic payment that required user software to withdraw notes from a bank and pick specific encrypted keys before sending them to a recipient. As a result, the digital money could not be traced by the issuing bank, the government, or another third party.

In 1996, the National Security Agency released a document titled How to Make a Mint: the Cryptography of Anonymous Electronic Cash, first on an MIT email list and then in The American Law Review in 1997, proposing a Cryptocurrency system. (Volume 46, Number 4)

Wei Dai described "b-money" as an anonymous, distributed electronic cash system in 1998. Nick Szabo soon after related bit gold. Bit gold (not to be confused with the subsequent gold-based exchange, BitGold) was characterized as an electronic money system that required users to fulfil proof of work function, with solutions cryptographically built and published, similar to bitcoin and other cryptocurrencies to come.

In 2009, Satoshi Nakamoto, a reportedly pseudonymous creator, created the first decentralized cryptocurrency, bitcoin. It utilized SHA-256, a cryptographic hash algorithm, in its proof-of-work mechanism. Namecoin was established in April 2011 to build a decentralized DNS that would make internet censorship very difficult. Soon after, in October 2011, Litecoin was introduced. It used scrypt as its hash method rather than SHA-256. Another important cryptocurrency, Peercoin, employs a proof-of-work/proof-of-stake hybrid.

On August 6, 2014, the UK Treasury announced that it had commissioned a study of cryptocurrencies and their potential role in the UK economy. The study was also expected to provide recommendations on whether or not regulation should be pursued. Its final report was published in 2018, and consultation on crypto assets and stable coins was initiated in January 2021.

El Salvador became the first country to recognize Bitcoin as legal tender in June 2021, when the Legislative Assembly approved a measure sponsored by President Nayib Bukele to classify the cryptocurrency as such by a vote of 62–22.

In August 2021, Cuba followed Resolution 215 to recognize and manage cryptocurrencies such as bitcoin.

The government of China, the world's largest cryptocurrency market, ruled all cryptocurrency transactions illegal in September 2021, completing a cryptocurrency crackdown that had previously restricted the operation of intermediaries and miners inside China.

HOW DO CRYPTOCURRENCIES FUNCTION?

The source codes and technological controls that enable and safeguard cryptocurrencies are, indeed, quite complicated. However, laypeople are more than capable of grasping the fundamental ideas and becoming knowledgeable bitcoin users.

Several ideas influence the values, security, and integrity of cryptocurrencies.

Cryptography Cryptocurrencies safeguard their exchange units using cryptographic protocols, which are incredibly complicated coding systems that encrypt sensitive data transfers.

Cryptocurrency developers create these protocols using complex mathematics and computer engineering concepts, making them hard to breach and thereby copy or counterfeit the secured coins.

These protocols also conceal bitcoin users' identities, making transactions and financial flows challenging to link to particular persons or organizations.

Blockchain Technology, The blockchain of a cryptocurrency is the master public database that records and preserves all previous transactions and activity, verifying ownership of all currency units at any one moment.

A blockchain is the record of a cryptocurrency's entire transaction history to date. It has a limited length — comprising a finite number of transactions — that grows over time.

Every node of the cryptocurrency's software network stores identical copies of the blockchain — the network of decentralized server farms maintained by computer-savvy people or groups known as miners who constantly record and confirm bitcoin transactions.

A bitcoin transaction is not technically complete until uploaded to the blockchain, which usually happens within minutes. When a transaction is completed, it is typically irrevocable.

Unlike standard payment processors such as PayPal and credit cards, most cryptocurrencies do not provide built-in refund or chargeback functionality, while some newer coins do.

The units are not accessible for either party during the lag period between the transaction's inception and completion. They are instead kept in escrow — limbo.

The blockchain, therefore, prohibits double-spending or the modification of bitcoin code to replicate and send the same money units to numerous receivers.

DECENTRALIZED CONTROL.

The notion of decentralized control is inherent in blockchain technology.

The quantity and value of cryptocurrencies are determined by the actions of their users and the very sophisticated procedures incorporated into their governing codes, rather than by deliberate choices made by central banks or other regulatory agencies.

The operations of miners, in particular, are essential to the stability and seamless operation of currencies. Miners are cryptocurrency users who employ huge quantities of computer power to record transactions in exchange for freshly produced cryptocurrency units and transaction fees paid by other users.

KEYS TO PRIVATE PLACES

Every cryptocurrency owner has a private key that enables them to trade units and validate their identity. In addition, users may generate their private keys, which are formatted as whole numbers up to 78 digits long, or utilize a random number generator.

They can get and spend bitcoin once they have a key. However, the possessor cannot spend or convert their bitcoin without the key, thereby declaring their assets useless until the key is retrieved.

While this is an important security feature that decreases theft and illegal usage, it is also quite harsh. Losing your private key is like tossing a bunch of cash into a garbage incinerator.

Although you may generate a new private key and begin collecting bitcoin again, you will be unable to retrieve the assets secured by your previous, lost key.

Savvy cryptocurrency users are therefore maniacally cautious of their private keys, routinely keeping them in various digital places — usually not Internet-connected for security reasons — as well as on paper or in another physical form.

CRYPTOCURRENCY MINING

Mining is the process of validating transactions in cryptocurrency networks. As a return for their efforts, prosperous miners get fresh bitcoin. The reward reduces transaction costs by giving a complementary incentive to contribute to the network's processing capacity. The usage of specialized devices like FPGAs and ASICs running complicated hashing algorithms such as SHA-256 and scrypt has enhanced the pace of creating hashes, which verify each transaction. Since the first cryptocurrency, bitcoin, in 2009, there has been an arms race for cheaper-yet-efficient equipment.

As more individuals enter the virtual currency realm, producing hashes for validation has gotten more sophisticated, pushing miners to spend increasingly significant amounts of money to enhance computational speed. As a result, the reward for discovering a hash has decreased and often does not justify the investment in equipment, cooling facilities (to limit the heat produced by the equipment), and the power necessary to operate them.

As a result, mining is prevalent in areas with cheap energy, a cold temperature, and governments with clear and friendly legislation. As of July 2019, bitcoin's power usage is predicted to be at seven gigatonnes, or 0.2 percent of the world total, or around the same as Switzerland's.

Some miners pool their resources, distributing their processing power across a network to share the reward evenly based on the amount of labor they contributed to the chance of discovering a block. Members of the mining pool who produce a valid partial proof-of-work get a "share."

As of February 2018, the Chinese government has suspended virtual currency trade, prohibited initial coin offerings, and shut off mining. Since then, many Chinese miners have migrated to Canada and Texas. Due to low gas costs, one business is establishing data centers for mining activities at Canadian oil and gas field locations. In June 2018, Hydro Quebec recommended to the provincial government that 500 MW be allocated to cryptocurrency mining businesses. According to a Fortune story from February 2018, [59] Iceland has become a refuge for bitcoin miners due to its inexpensive power.

To protect natural resources and the cities "character and direction," the mayor of Plattsburgh in upstate New York imposed an 18-month embargo on any cryptocurrency mining in March 2018.

Miners function as record keepers for cryptocurrency communities and indirect arbiters of the currencies' worth.

Miners employ huge quantities of processing power, frequently embodied in private server farms operated by mining collectives comprised of hundreds of people, to check the completeness, correctness, and security of currencies' blockchains.

The scale of the process is similar to the hunt for new prime numbers, which similarly requires massive quantities of computational power.

Miners' activity makes fresh copies of the blockchain regularly, including recent, previously unconfirmed transactions that haven't been included in any prior blockchain copy – thus completing such transactions.

Each addition is referred to as a block. Blocks are made up of all transactions since the previous fresh copy of the blockchain was produced.

The word "miners" refers to the fact that the labor of miners physically produces money in the form of new bitcoin units.

In reality, each freshly produced blockchain copy comes with a two-part monetary reward: a set number of newly minted ("mined") cryptocurrency units and a variable number of existing units collected via optional transaction fees paid by purchasers (usually less than 1% of the transaction value).

It's worth mentioning that cryptocurrency mining was once a potentially profitable side business for individuals with the means to engage in power- and hardware-intensive mining operations.

Today, it is unfeasible for enthusiasts to invest in professional-grade mining equipment unless they have thousands of dollars to spare. However, suppose you only want to augment your regular income. In that case, many freelancing opportunities can pay you more.

Although sellers are not charged transaction fees, miners can favor fee-loaded transactions over fee-free transactions when producing new blocks, even if the fee-free transactions occurred earlier.

Because sellers have an incentive to charge transaction fees because they are paid quicker, it's extremely usual for bitcoin transactions to include costs.

Although it is theoretically feasible for previously unconfirmed transactions on a fresh blockchain copy to be fee-free, this nearly never occurs in reality.

Cryptocurrencies automatically react to the amount of mining power working to produce new blockchain copies through instructions in its source code – copies become more challenging to make as mining power grows and more straightforward to create as mining power lowers.

The idea is to maintain a constant average interval between fresh blockchain developments. For example, Bitcoin's is 10 minutes.

CRYPTOCURRENCY TRADING

Trading is a fundamental economic concept that involves purchasing and selling assets. These may be commodities or services, with the buyer compensating the vendor. In addition, the transaction may entail the trade partners exchanging products and services in other circumstances.

The assets being exchanged in the financial markets are referred to as financial instruments. Examples are stocks, bonds, and currency pairings on the Forex market, options, futures, margin products, cryptocurrencies, and many more. Don't worry if you're unfamiliar with these phrases; we'll go over them all later in this post.

Short-term trading, in which traders actively enter and leave positions over relatively short periods, is generally referred to as trading. This, however, is a bit deceptive assumption. Trading, in reality, may relate to a wide variety of tactics, including day trading, swing trading, trend trading, and many more. But don't be concerned. We'll go through each of these in further depth later.

Investing is the process of allocating resources (such as capital) with the expectation of profit. This might include using money to develop and launch a business or acquiring property with the idea of reselling it at a higher price later on. This generally comprises buying financial assets to sell them at a higher price later in the financial markets.

The expectation of a return is fundamental to the investing concept (also known as R.O.I.). As opposed to trading, investing often employs a longer-term approach to wealth growth. An investor's goal is to amass wealth over a long period (years or even decades). There are numerous approaches to this, but most investors will depend on fundamental factors to uncover potentially successful investment opportunities.

Investors are usually unfazed by short-term market movements due to the long-term nature of their approach. Consequently, they are frequently relatively passive, not worried about short-term losses.

WHAT'S THE DIFFERENCE BETWEEN TRADING AND INVESTING?

Traders, as well as investors, seek profits in the financial markets. But, on the other hand, their ways to reach this goal are opposed.

In general, investors want to generate a return over a more extended period, such as years or even decades. Therefore, investors' projected returns on each investment are often more significant since they have a longer time horizon.

Traders, on the other hand, seek to benefit from market volatility. As a result, they are more likely to enter and exit positions. In addition, they may seek smaller returns on each trade (since they constantly enter several transactions).

Which is superior? Which one is better suited to you? That is all up to you. You may begin by educating yourself about markets, and then you can learn by doing. You'll be able to discover which one best matches your financial objectives, personality, and trading profile over time.

HOW TO PROFIT FROM CRYPTOCURRENCY

If you're wondering how to make money using bitcoin, look no further!

Making money with bitcoin is accomplished via three mechanisms:

To begin, you might invest or trade in the bitcoin exchange market. This is possible without holding any cryptocurrencies, just as investing in gold on the stock market is possible.

Second, you may use your present money to stake and lend coins to the system or other users.

Finally, you may contribute to the blockchain system by mining or earning monetary rewards for system effort.

Based on these three principles, below are the six strategies for producing money using cryptocurrencies:

- ❖ Investing
- ❖ Trading
- ❖ Staking and Lending
- ❖ Crypto Social Media
- ❖ Mining

❖ Airdrops and Forks

Each of these strategies is explored in more detail below.

1. Making an investment

Investing is a long-term strategy that involves acquiring and holding crypto assets for a prolonged time. Crypto assets, in general, are best suited to a buy-and-hold strategy. This is because they are quite volatile in the short term, but they have great long-term growth potential.

The investment strategy demands selecting more dependable assets that will last long. Long-term price gains in assets such as Bitcoin and Ethereum have been seen, making them a safe investment in this respect.

2. Trading

Unlike investing, a long-term strategy based on buy-and-hold, trading is meant to profit on short-term opportunities.

The bitcoin market is a very volatile one. This means that the values of assets may vary dramatically in a short period.

To be a successful trader, you must possess excellent analytical and technical skills. To make accurate predictions about price increases and falls, you'll need to evaluate market charts based on the performance of the listed assets.

When trading, you may take a long or short position based on whether you believe an asset's price will climb or decline. This implies you may earn whether the cryptocurrency market is bullish or negative.

Check out our day trading crypto guide to learn more about the cryptocurrency market.

3. Lending and investing

Staking is a technique for validating bitcoin transactions. You have coins but do not utilize them when you bet. The coins are instead kept in a cryptocurrency wallet. Your currencies are then used to validate transactions on a Proof of Stake network. You will be rewarded for your efforts. You are, in essence, lending coins to the network. This enables the network to maintain its security and to validate transactions. The advantage is akin to the interest you get from a bank on a credit balance.

The Proof of Stake algorithm chooses transaction validators depending on the number of coins staked. This makes it significantly more energy-efficient than crypto mining and eliminates the need for costly equipment.

You may also make money by lending coins to other investors. Crypto financing is made feasible by several sites.

To understand more, see our lending cryptocurrency guide.

4. Cryptography The Internet of Things (IoT)

You will be compensated for creating and curating content for several blockchain-based social media networks. In addition, you are often rewarded with the platform's currency.

5. Mining

Cryptocurrency mining makes money using cryptocurrency in the same manner that the early pioneers did. Mining is a key component of the Proof of Work technique. It is the source of the value of a cryptocurrency.

If you mine a cryptocurrency, you will be rewarded with new coins. However, mining requires both technical knowledge and initial investment in specialized technology.

Mining is a subset of master node administration. It requires expertise as well as significant upfront and ongoing dedication.

6. Airdrops and Forks

Airdrops and free tokens are distributed to boost awareness. For example, an exchange may launch an airdrop to increase the number of users for a project. In addition, participating in an airdrop may provide you with free cash that you may use to buy stuff, invest in, or trade with.

When a protocol changes or improves, it causes a blockchain split, resulting in new money creation. If you have coins on the old chain, you will often get free tokens on the new network. This implies you receive a free coin for being at the correct place at the right moment.

___

Chapter 2

WHAT EXACTLY IS AN NFT?

You'd have to be living under a rock to have missed the latest NFT (non-fungible token) craze. Celebrities, digital artists, and creatives are all preparing to publish their work on the blockchain.

When it comes to minting NFTs, the choices are endless, ranging from artworks to melodies to collectible N.B.A. trade cards. It's an excellent technique to demonstrate the authenticity and ownership of creative works.

If you're very skilled (or fortunate), you can earn a good living. Consider it a digital valuable record or a one-of-a-kind artwork. If there is a great demand for your NFT, costs might skyrocket. You may be familiar with visual artist

Beeple, who sold an NFT titled "Everyday: the First 5000 Days" for more than $69 million.

In addition to Beeple, other artists are selling their NFTs on blockchain-based markets. But, again, the best-selling items speak for themselves.

A non-fungible token (NFT) is a digital asset that can be validated using blockchain technology. Artwork, music, and in-game assets such as different avatars are examples. Because they are one-of-a-kind, NFTs are gaining popularity as collectors.

NFT is an abbreviation for 'non-fungible token.' When something, such as a dollar bill, is fungible, it is comparable and may be traded for any other $1 note. A non-fungible token, on the other hand, is a one-of-a-kind digital asset that cannot be exchanged for another NFT. As a result, each NFT is a 'one-of-a-kind' piece. NFTs are transferred from one owner to another via blockchain technology, which generates a digital trail from the seller to the buyer that confirms the transaction. This encodes the buyer's exclusive ownership rights (new owner).

The physical world equivalent would be a one-of-a-kind collectable item, such as a work of art, for which you would have a certificate of ownership attesting to its authenticity. The NFT, with its blockchain technology, eliminates the requirement for ownership certificates. Instead, certain

NFTs employ blockchain technology to establish a digital ownership certificate for a unique physical object, albeit this is not widely used at the moment.

Even though they have been present since 2014, NFTs became a popular investment in 2021. As the popularity of cryptocurrency investment grew, so did the concept of offering specific digital assets to investors for purchase online.

HOW DO NFTS WORK?

Online markets such as Rarity.tools and NFTcatcher.io advertise and distribute NFTs. Investors may browse an inventory of assets before deciding which one to purchase. To purchase the digital asset, one needs to have a cryptocurrency and set up an account on the marketplace linked to the cryptocurrency wallet containing the coins.

Ethereum ERC-20 tokens are the most commonly used blockchain NFT tokens. The ERC-20 token is what the Ethereum network utilizes to launch a smart contract. NFTs may also be acquired with Polygon, Solana, and Polkadot coins.

NFTs have provided a new avenue for artists, businesses, and celebrities to monetize their assets. Artists may establish a library of digital goods to sell to a new generation of investors and collectors. Celebrities are developing assets that leverage their famous brand identity. Some NFTs are worth hundreds, if not millions, of dollars.

WHAT IS THE DIFFERENCE BETWEEN NFTS AND CRYPTOCURRENCY?

NFTs and bitcoin are not the same things. The transaction is carried out via an NFT using bitcoins. It uses the same blockchain technology as bitcoin, but the asset is structured differently. The NFT, unlike a cryptocurrency token, cannot be traded or swapped at equivalency. Instead, each cryptographic asset is assigned a unique identification number and information differentiating one NFT from another. In other words, you may exchange one Bitcoin for another — they are equal – but NFTs do not.

HOW TO INVEST IN NFTS

Purchasing NFTs necessitates the investor's or collectors due diligence. You must first choose NFTs that you believe will appreciate the value and are interested in collecting.

You may learn more about NFTs by looking through the many markets that conduct sales and auctions. You may also participate in NFT Discord and Telegram discussions to discover other people's opinions about existing NFTs and forthcoming releases.

You cannot buy an NFT unless you have a bitcoin wallet. This means you must first acquire the cryptocurrency necessary for the transaction using a brokerage service like Coinbase (NASDAQ: COIN) or Robinhood (NASDAQ: HOOD) and connect the cryptocurrency wallet that houses your cryptocurrency to the marketplace where you plan to purchase the NFT.

HOW TO DESIGN YOUR NFTS

The Binance NFT Marketplace is an excellent place to start if you want to construct your own NFTs. You can also do it directly on the Binance Smart Chain (B.S.C.) by using Defi platforms such as Featured by Binance, BakerySwap, or TreasureLand. B.S.C. has a thriving NFT community, cheap fees, and speedy transaction times.

There are several sites to pick from, but most need you to enter your NFT data, submit your digital art or file, and pay the minting price. If you want to sell your NFT, you may do so swiftly on various NFT markets.

WHAT KIND OF BLOCKCHAIN SHOULD I USE?

There are various blockchains to choose from when minting an NFT. In their present form, non-fungible tokens were introduced by the Ethereum network as the first substantial blockchain. NFT support has been added to Binance Smart Chain, Polkadot, Tron, Tezos, and many more blockchains.

The bulk of NFTs is now based on Ethereum or B.S.C. However, the high cost of Ethereum's gas has made minting and maintaining NFTs extremely expensive. Binance Smart Chain is a much less costly solution with a faster transaction speed. In addition, there are various NFT marketplaces and projects, giving you access to a large number of prospective customers.

WHAT PLATFORM SHOULD I USE TO BUILD NFTS?

Choosing a platform to mint your NFT is a question of personal taste as well as the blockchain you want to use. However, because most B.S.C. protocols produce your NFT as a BEP-721 token, they will end up being the same regardless of whatever protocol you choose.

Suppose you want to trade your token later quickly. In that case, it's usually preferable to use a platform with a marketplace you're already acquainted with. You won't have to move your NFT to a separate location after minting it this method.

We prefer BakerySwap and Treasureland for their simplicity of use. All of these B.S.C. initiatives provide easy-to-use interfaces and low costs for minting your NFT. BakerySwap is the biggest NFT marketplace, making it an excellent alternative for anybody looking to sell their NFT after minting. Treasureland allows you to create NFTs for free. If you're thinking about employing Ethereum, two of the most popular solutions are OpenSea and Rarible.

Chapter 3

METAVERSE

Financial, virtual, and real worlds have become more linked. The technology we use to govern our lives provides us access to almost anything we want at the touch of a button. This has also had an impact on the cryptocurrency business. NFTs, blockchain games, and cryptocurrency payments are no longer limited to cryptocurrency enthusiasts. They're all now publicly available as part of the expanding metaverse.

The metaverse is a 3D online virtual realm that connects individuals in all parts of their life. It would link several platforms, similar to how the internet connects various websites accessed with a single browser.

Neal Stephenson's science-fiction book Snow Crash introduced the notion. However, although the concept of a metaverse was initially considered fiction, it now seems that it may become a reality in the future.

Augmented reality will power the metaverse, with each user managing a character or avatar. So, for example, you might have a mixed reality conference in your virtual workplace using an Oculus V.R. headset, conclude work and relax in a blockchain-based game, and then manage your crypto portfolio and finances all inside the metaverse.

The financial, virtual, and physical worlds have grown more intertwined. The technology we use to regulate our lives allows us to get practically everything we desire with the press of a button. This has also affected the bitcoin industry. NFTs, blockchain games, and cryptocurrency payments are no longer exclusive to cryptocurrency enthusiasts. They're all now open to the public as part of the ever-expanding metaverse. Unfortunately, the metaverse does not yet exist.

The metaverse will enable economics, digital identification, decentralized government, and other uses in addition to games and social media. Even today, user production and ownership of valuable goods and currencies contribute to developing a unified metaverse. All of these characteristics give blockchain the ability to fuel this future technology.

WHAT EXACTLY IS THE METAVERSE?

The metaverse is an idea of a permanent, online, 3D cosmos that integrates many virtual places. Consider it a future iteration of the internet. Thanks to the metaverse, users will collaborate, meet, game, and interact in these 3D environments.

The metaverse does not yet exist in its entirety; however, several platforms feature metaverse-like aspects. At the moment, video games give the closest metaverse experience available. Developers have stretched the definition of a game by organizing in-game events and building virtual economies.

Cryptocurrencies, although not needed, may be an excellent match for a metaverse. They enable the creation of a digital economy via various utility tokens and virtual collectibles (NFTs). Adopting crypto wallets such as Trust Wallet and MetaMask would also improve the metaverse. Furthermore, blockchain technology can establish transparent and dependable governance structures.

Existing blockchain-based, metaverse-like apps offer individuals with livable earnings. For example, Axie Infinity is a popular play-to-earn game that many people use to supplement their income. SecondLife and Decentraland are two more instances of blockchain and virtual reality applications.

In the future, huge I.T. companies are attempting to set the pace. However, the decentralized nature of the blockchain sector allows smaller players to create the metaverse as well.

WHAT IS THE SIGNIFICANCE OF VIDEO GAMES IN THE METAVERSE?

Because of the emphasis on 3D virtual reality, video games are currently the closest to a metaverse experience. This isn't only because they're in 3D. Video games rapidly provide services and features that may be used in numerous aspects of our lives. Roblox, a computer game, even offers virtual events like concerts and meetings. Players no longer only play the game; they also use it for other activities and elements of their lives in "cyberspace." For example, Travis Scott's virtual in-game music tour garnered 12.3 million Fortnite gamers.

WHAT IS THE FUNCTION OF CRYPTOCURRENCIES IN THE METAVERSE?

Gaming provides the 3D component of the metaverse. Still, it does not provide all needed in a virtual world that may cover all aspects of life. Other key elements, such as digital proof of ownership, value transfer, governance, and accessibility, may be provided by cryptocurrency. But what exactly do these phrases imply?

We'll need a secure system to establish ownership if we work, communicate, and even purchase virtual items in the metaverse in the future. We must also feel safe while transporting goods and money throughout the metaverse. Finally, since the metaverse will be an essential part of our lives, we'll want to participate in the decision-making process.

Some video games already have rudimentary solutions, but many creators employ crypto and blockchain as superior choices. While video game development is more tightly managed, blockchain allows for a decentralized and transparent way to deal with challenges.

The video game industry also has an impact on blockchain developers. Gamification is used in both Decentralized Finance (Defi) and GameFi. There seem to be enough commonalities for the two worlds to become even more intertwined in the future. The essential qualities of blockchain that make it ideal for the metaverse are as follows:

1. **Digital proof of ownership:** If you have access to your private keys via a wallet, you may instantly verify ownership of a blockchain action or asset. To show accountability, you might, for example, give an accurate transcript of your blockchain transactions while at work. A wallet is one of the most secure and dependable in-game methods of creating a digital identity and proof of ownership.

2. **Digital collectability:** Just as we can determine who owns something, we can also demonstrate that an object is original and one-of-a-kind. This is critical for a metaverse that wants to include more real-life activities. We may use NFTs to construct unique and cannot be replicated or fabricated. A blockchain may also reflect actual object ownership.

3. **Value transfer:** A metaverse will need a safe transfer method that users can depend on. The in-game currency in multiplayer games is less secure than blockchain-based crypto. Suppose people spend a significant amount of time in the metaverse and even make money

there. In that case, they will need a trustworthy currency.

4. **Governance:** Users should manage the laws of their interactions with the metaverse. We can vote in corporations and elect leaders and governments in real life. The metaverse will also need methods for implementing fair governance, and blockchain is currently a proven method for doing so.

5. **Accessibility:** Anyone in the world may create a wallet on public blockchains. Unlike a bank account, you are not required to pay any money or submit any information. As a result, it is one of the most accessible managing funds and online digital identities.

6. **Interoperability:** Blockchain technology is constantly increasing platform compatibility. Polkadot (D.O.T.) and Avalanche (A.V.A.X.) projects enable the creation of unique blockchains that can communicate with one another. A single metaverse will be required to link different initiatives, and blockchain technology has already provided answers for this.

WHAT IS A METAVERSE JOB?

As previously said, the metaverse will bring all facets of existence together in one area. While many individuals now work from home, you will be able to visit a 3D workplace and engage with your coworkers' avatars in the metaverse. Your employment might potentially be metaverse-related, providing you with revenue that you can use in the metaverse. In reality, employment of this kind already exists in some manner.

People throughout the globe now have consistent revenue streams because of GameFi and play-to-earn models. These online occupations are excellent candidates for future metaverse implementation because they demonstrate that individuals are ready to spend time living and earning in virtual environments. Axie Infinity and Gods Unchained are two examples of play-to-earn games that lack 3D settings and avatars. However, it is the notion that they might be a part of the metaverse to make money entirely online.

EXAMPLES OF THE METAVERSE

While there is no one connected metaverse yet, several platforms and initiatives are analogous to the metaverse.

Typically, they include NFTs and other blockchain components. Consider the following three examples:

1. SecondLife

SecondLife is a three-dimensional virtual world where users control avatars for socializing, learning, and business. There is also an NFT marketplace for trading collectibles in the project. As part of its one anniversary, SecondLife will host Binance Smart Chain's Harvest Festival in September 2020. The virtual exhibition allowed users to explore and engage with various initiatives in the B.S.C. ecosystem.

2. Infinite Axie

Axie Infinity is a play-to-earn game that allows users in developing nations to earn a constant income. A player may begin farming the Smooth Love Potion (S.L.P.) token by buying or being given three Axis. Depending on how much they play and the market price, someone may profit between $200 and $1000 (USD) by selling their tickets on the open market.

While Axie Infinity does not offer a single 3D character or avatar, it does provide users with the chance to work in a metaverse-like environment. You may have heard the well-known stories of Filipinos adopting it as an alternative to full-time jobs or assistance.

3. Decentraland

Decentraland is a virtual realm that mixes social aspects with cryptocurrencies, NFTs, and virtual real estate. Furthermore, participants participate actively in the platform's governance. NFTs represent cosmetic collectibles in blockchain games, as they are in other blockchain games. They're also utilized for LAND, which are 16x16 meter land parcels that players may buy in the game using the cryptocurrency MANA. All of these factors combine to form a complicated crypto-economy.

WHAT IS THE METAVERSE FUTURE?

Facebook is one of the most vocal proponents of a united metaverse. Because of Facebook's Diem stablecoin project, this is very intriguing for a crypto-powered metaverse. Mark Zuckerberg has intended to create a metaverse initiative to facilitate remote employment and provide financial prospects for individuals in underdeveloped nations. Because Facebook has social media, communication, and cryptocurrency platforms, it has a solid start in merging all of these realms into one. Microsoft, Apple, and Google are among the other significant I.T. corporations aiming to build a metaverse.

Further integration between NFT markets and 3D virtual environments seems the next stage toward a crypto-powered metaverse. NFT holders may already sell their items from various sources on markets such as OpenSea and BakerySwap. Still, there is no widespread 3D platform for this. Blockchain developers may create popular metaverse-like applications with more organic users than a large tech behemoth on a larger scale.

Chapter 4

PLAY-TO-EARN GAMES

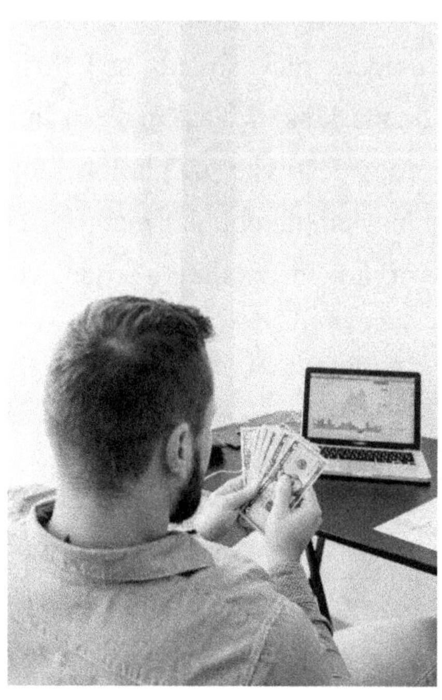

Throughout the 50-year history of home video gaming, games have served as a distraction, something to distract you from a long day's work. However, a new generation of video games is employing blockchain technology such as NFTs to reward players with bitcoin.

These "play-to-earn" games are already allowing gamers to do a job by playing video games in certain nations, with scholarship programs and academies cropping up to assist players in navigating this weird new world.

While some have welcomed the introduction of play-to-earn games, saying that they allow players to earn incentives for doing something they would have done for free before, many gamers have voiced concern about the unwanted incursion of commerce into the escapist world of gaming.

WHAT EXACTLY ARE PLAY-TO-EARN GAMES?

Described, play-to-earn games are video games where the player may earn real-world benefits.

While individuals have been making money from video games for many years via methods such as "gold farming" and unauthorized markets for in-game goods, the advent of blockchain technology and NFTs have essentially transformed the game.

Non-fungible tokens, or NFTs, are cryptographically distinct tokens that may be used to establish ownership of material such as photographs or music. They let players assume ownership of in-game assets such as virtual apparel or plots of land in blockchain games.

Unlike traditional games, in which in-game objects are kept on closed data networks and controlled by the corporations who produced the game, NFTs allow users to own the unique assets they acquire. Furthermore, if you possess the NFT, you may freely sell it outside of the platform it was developed, which is not feasible with traditional games.

That is, NFTs representing in-game items may be bought and sold for fiat money on any NFT marketplace. However, due to the scarcity of such NFTs, they have real-world value.

There is no purpose to playing typical games other than for pure enjoyment. The link is one-sided: you pay for the game, and unless you are a professional esports player or a streamer with a significant following, you will never be able to monetize your playing. On the other hand, Blockchain gaming enables players to make real money.

Players may transfer value and get paid to play regardless of who they are or global since blockchain technology allows users to trade wherever they are.

THE EMERGENCE OF PLAY-TO-EARN

With 2.8 million daily players and a total transaction volume of $3.8 billion, Axie Infinity has become one of the most popular play-to-earn games, with individuals in countries like the Philippines and Indonesia even using Axie to support their families. In addition, "Axie scholarship" schemes, such as Yield Guild Games, have also evolved, allowing Axie owners to lend their NFTs to other players.

According to Axie Infinity co-founder Aleksander Leonard Larsen, half of the game's players had never used a cryptocurrency before. However, there are costs connected with playing the game, and you must first get three Axie NFTs, which may cost hundreds of dollars apiece. In addition, Larsen acknowledged the problems attracting new players, saying, "It's tough to start playing Axie right now." To address this problem, Axie plans to provide free starting Axis with limited earning potential to attract new players to the game.

Other play-to-earn systems integrate NFT games with decentralized financial components (Defi). For example, Aavegotchi, a Defi money market Aave-funded experiment, allows users to stake Aave's tokens inside cartoon creatures represented by NFT's, suggesting that each Aavegotchi generates Aave yield.

The potential of NFTs and play-to-earn has also grabbed the attention of the mainstream gaming industry; Ubisoft, a French video game firm, has already disclosed plans for Ubisoft Quartz, a platform that lets players earn and purchase NFTs based on the Tezos blockchain. However, other publishers experimenting with NFTs have received a hostile reaction from players, with S.T.A.L.K.E.R. 2 developer G.S.C. Game World abandoning plans to include NFTs after a player-led Twitter campaign.

Some players, already frustrated by publishers' commercialization of games via "pay-to-win" models and loot boxes, perceive play-to-earn as going too far, believing that incorporating real-world economic models and incentives would turn gaming from an escape into a capitalist "investment" industry.

However, with companies like F.T.X. and Andreesen Horowitz pouring money into the play-to-earn market, it shows no signs of slowing down anytime soon.

———————————

Chapter 5

DECENTRALIZED FINANCE (DEFI)

WHAT IS IT?

Decentralized finance (Defi) is a new financial system built on secure distributed ledgers, similar to those used by cryptocurrencies. The system eliminates banks' and institutions' control over money, financial goods, and financial services.

One of the most appealing aspects of Defi for many customers is that it removes the costs that banks and other financial institutions charge for utilizing their services.

Instead of holding your money in a bank, you store it in a secure digital wallet, which anybody with an internet connection may use without requiring clearance, and which allows you to move payments in seconds or minutes.

DECENTRALIZED FINANCE EXPLAINED (DEFI)

To comprehend decentralized finance and how it works, it is necessary to understand how it differs from centralized finance. Finance is centralized.

Banks, companies whose ultimate objective is to earn money, hold your money under centralized finance. Third parties that enable money flow between parties abound in the financial system, with each demanding a charge for their services. For example, assume you use your credit card to buy a gallon of milk. The charge is routed from the merchant to an acquiring bank, passing the card information to the credit card network.

The network clears the charge and asks your bank for payment. Your bank accepts the charge, forwards it to the network, and then delivers it to the merchant through the acquiring bank. Each organization in the chain is compensated for its services, mainly because retailers must compensate you for your ability to use credit and debit cards.

All other financial activities are costly; loan applications might take days to be accepted, and you may be unable to utilize a bank's services if you are traveling.

FINANCE IS DECENTRALIZED.

Decentralized finance reduces the need for intermediaries by enabling individuals, merchants, and organizations to execute financial transactions using developing technologies. This is performed using peer-to-peer financial networks that use security protocols, connection, software and hardware improvements, etc.

You may lend, trade, and borrow using software that records and validates financial transactions in distributed financial databases from wherever you have an internet connection. A distributed database is accessible from several places; it gathers and aggregates data from all users and verifies it using a consensus process.

Decentralized finance makes use of this technology to abolish centralized finance models by allowing anybody, regardless of who or where they are, to utilize financial services everywhere.

Defi apps provide users greater control over their money through personal wallets and trade services tailored to people.

WHAT IS THE PROCESS OF DEFI?

Decentralized finance uses the same blockchain technology as cryptocurrencies. A blockchain is a distributed and secure database, often known as a ledger. To process transactions and manage the blockchain, applications known as dApps are utilized.

Transactions are recorded in blocks on the blockchain and confirmed by other users. If these verifiers agree on a transaction, the block is closed and encrypted. Then, a new block is created with information about the previous block.

The information in each successive block "chains" the blocks together, thus the word blockchain. There is no method to modify a blockchain since information in previous blocks cannot be changed without affecting later ones. In conjunction with other security processes, this strategy adds to the blockchain's secure nature.

DEFI IN THE FUTURE

The development of decentralized finance is still in its early stages. To begin with, it is unregulated, which means the ecosystem is still plagued with infrastructure problems, hacks, and scams.

The current legal framework is based on different financial jurisdictions, each with its own set of rules and regulations. The ability of Defi to undertake borderless transactions poses serious concerns for this kind of legislation. For example, who is responsible for investigating a financial crime across borders, protocols, and Defi apps? Who would be in charge of enforcing the regulations, and how would they be done?

System stability, energy needs, carbon footprint, system updates, system maintenance, and hardware failures are further considerations.

Many problems must be solved, and advances must be made before Defi may be used safely. However, financial institutions will not give up one of their key sources of revenue if Defi succeeds. Moreover, if Defi succeeds, banks and businesses will find methods to get into the system, if not to control how you access your money, then to profit from it.

Chapter 6

THE CRYPTO FUTURE

Some economic experts believe that institutional money will join the cryptocurrency market, causing a significant shift in the market. Furthermore, there is a chance that crypto may be listed on the NASDAQ, which would provide legitimacy to blockchain and its applications as an alternative to traditional currencies.

Some believe that all cryptocurrencies need a confirmed exchange-traded fund (ETF). An ETF would undoubtedly make it simpler for consumers to invest in Bitcoin. However, there must still be a desire to invest in cryptocurrency, which a fund may not produce automatically.

Some of the existing limitations of cryptocurrencies, such as the fact that a computer crash might erase one's digital riches or that a hacker can rob a virtual vault, may be overcome in the future by technological developments. However, what will be more challenging to overcome is the fundamental paradox that cryptocurrencies confront. As they get more popular, they are likely to encounter more regulation and government inspection, weakening the essential premise for their existence.

While the number of retailers accepting cryptocurrency has constantly climbed, they remain a small percentage. To become more extensively utilized, cryptocurrencies must first earn significant consumer approval. However, their considerable complexity compared to traditional currencies will likely repel most individuals, except the technologically savvy.

A cryptocurrency that seeks to be a part of the mainstream financial system may be required to meet wildly disparate standards. For example, it would need to be mathematically complex (to prevent fraud and hacker attacks), but simple for consumers to understand; decentralized, but with adequate consumer safeguards and protection; and maintain user anonymity without acting as a conduit for tax evasion, money laundering, and other nefarious activities Given how difficult these conditions are to meet, is it feasible that the most popular cryptocurrency in a few years would have characteristics that lie between severely controlled fiat currencies and today's cryptocurrencies? While that prospect is improbable, there is no question that, as the primary cryptocurrency at the moment, Bitcoin's success (or failure) in dealing with the problems it confronts may decide the fortunes of other cryptocurrencies in the years ahead.

———————————